INSIGHT INTO SLEEP PARALYSIS

A Holistic Approach to Understanding Sleep Paralysis and Related Sleep Conditions

Jean M. Clark

Table of Contents

Chapter 1

<u>SLEEP PARALYSIS DEFINED</u>

Sleep paralysis is a brief absence of muscle control soon after falling asleep or before waking up.

Sleep paralysis typically comprises hallucinations or a feeling of suffocation. No one understands exactly what causes sleep paralysis, but it is linked to sleep disorders and certain mental health conditions.

People whose sleep-wake cycles are disturbed by jet lag or shift work may be at higher risk for sleep paralysis.

While the states of sleep and waking are generally well-defined and distinct, conditions like sleep paralysis can obfuscate these boundaries.

Sleep paralysis is a momentary incapacity to move or talk that occurs directly after falling asleep or waking up. Individuals maintain consciousness throughout episodes, which generally entail terrible hallucinations and a sensation of suffocation.

Episodes of sleep paralysis involve aspects of both sleep and awake, which is mainly why they can lead to distressing symptoms. While much is still unknown about sleep paralysis, understanding about the sorts, symptoms, causes, consequences, and therapy could give a better awareness of the problem and ways to prevent it.

Sleep paralysis is a disorder described by a momentary absence of muscle control, known as atonia, that arises soon after falling asleep or before waking up. In addition to atonia, patients often have hallucinations during bouts of sleep paralysis.

Sleep paralysis is called parasomnia, which is an abnormal activity during sleep. Because it is linked to the rapid eye movement (REM) component of the sleep cycle, sleep paralysis is believed to constitute REM parasomnia.

Standard REM sleep contains vivid dreaming along with atonia, which usually helps prevent acting out dreams. Atonia generally ends upon waking up, hence a person never becomes mindful of this incapacity to move.

As a result, researchers believe that sleep paralysis implies a mixed state of consciousness that mixes both alertness and REM sleep. In effect, the atonia and mental images of REM sleep seem to continue even into a state of being cognizant and awake.

<u>SYMPTOMS OF SLEEP PARALYSIS</u>

Sleep paralysis is a confused sleep disorder characterised by a temporary incapacity to move or talk, often occurring either when falling asleep (hypnagogic sleep paralysis) or upon waking up (hypnopompic sleep paralysis).

This peculiar condition can be frightening and terrifying for persons who experience it, as they may stay alert and aware of their surroundings despite being immobile. Let's dig thoroughly into the symptoms of sleep paralysis, studying the physical and sensory manifestations, as well as the psychological influence it might have on affected folks.

1. Immobility and Muscle Weakness: One of the major indications of sleep paralysis is the entire or partial paralysis of voluntary muscles. During REM sleep (when most dreaming occurs), the brainstem generates chemicals that block muscle activity to prevent us from acting out our dreams.

This momentary paralysis is a regular component of the sleep cycle and helps to protect us from potential injury when dreaming.

However, in sleep paralysis, this muscle inhibition happens during waking or the transition between sleep stages, leaving the individual cognizant but unable to move. The perception of paralysis is frequently accompanied with a feeling of heaviness or pressure on the body, making it difficult to lift arms, legs, or even turn the head.

2. Consciousness and Awareness: Unlike normal sleep-related movement disorders, such as sleepwalking, patients experiencing sleep paralysis are entirely alert and aware of their surroundings.

Their cognitive faculties are intact, and they may be able to see, hear, and even think clearly. This heightened awareness throughout the incident leads to the feeling of vulnerability and terror.

3. Hallucinations: One of the most alarming symptoms of sleep paralysis is the occurrence of vivid hallucinations. These hallucinations can assume numerous shapes and affect different sensory modalities, including visual, auditory, tactile, and even smell feelings.

- <u>Visual Hallucinations:</u> Individuals may see shadowy figures, silhouettes, or odd, ethereal shapes in their surrounding area or approaching their bed. Some think encountering harmful or evil spirits results in a sensation of approaching peril.

- <u>Auditory Hallucinations:</u> Auditory experiences during sleep paralysis can range from hearing distant sounds, murmurs, or vague voices to loud, unpleasant noises or even shouting.

- <u>Tactile Hallucinations:</u> Some persons report feeling a sensation of pressure or being touched by unseen hands, a feeling of floating or levitating, or experiencing vibrations or electrical-like currents running through their body.

4. Distorted Perception of Time: During sleep paralysis, individuals often remark that the event feels much longer than it lasts. A few seconds or minutes can subjectively feel like a lifetime, intensifying the discomfort and anxiety related to the event.

5. Fear and Anxiety: The feeling of immobility, coupled with the prevalence of hallucinations, often causes a strong emotional response, particularly fear and anxiety.

This emotional reaction is further heightened by the brain's activation of the fight-or-flight response, which can be triggered when the mind perceives a threat even in the absence of genuine danger.

6. Impaired Breathing and Sensations of Choking: In rare cases, patients experiencing sleep paralysis may have difficulties breathing or feeling as if their breath is being choked. This impression of choking or suffocating can be worrisome, but it is crucial to remember that it is a subjective perception and not an actual medical concern.

7. Inability to Speak: While some folks may be able to make modest vocalisations or mumble during sleep paralysis, the majority find themselves unable to talk or shout out for relief, thereby contributing to the sense of helplessness.

8. Sleep Paralysis Disorder: For most people, sleep paralysis occurs occasionally and is not a cause for concern. However, for some individuals, sleep paralysis can become a persistent and troubling problem, hurting their quality of life and general well-being. In such instances, it may be classified as "Sleep Paralysis Disorder," a disorder that demands research and subsequent treatment by a healthcare professional or sleep specialist.

In many instances, these two distinguishing features are linked to generate a disease called recurrent isolated sleep paralysis (RISP), which contains continuous bouts of sleep paralysis in someone who does not have narcolepsy.

The defining indication of sleep paralysis is atonia, or the inability to move the body or talk. People also suffer problems breathing, chest tightness, and severe emotions like panic or helplessness during sleep paralysis episodes. It is typical to feel unduly tired or weary the day after having sleep paralysis.

Infographic demonstrating the 3 sorts of hallucinations: invasion hallucinations, chest pressure hallucinations, and vestibular-motor hallucinations.

An estimated 75% of sleep paralysis episodes also contain hallucinations that are unusual from ordinary dreams. These can occur as hypnagogic hallucinations when falling asleep or as hypnopompic hallucinations when waking up.

Hallucinations during sleep paralysis come into three kinds.

Intruder hallucinations: These hallucinations entail the impression of a menacing person or presence in the room.

Chest pressure hallucinations: Also called incubus hallucinations, these episodes may create symptoms of suffocation or the impression that someone is sitting on your chest. These frequently occur in combination with intruder hallucinations.

Vestibular-motor (V-M) hallucinations: V-M hallucinations could involve experiences of movement, such as flight, or out-of-body sensations.

Does Sleep Paralysis Have a Meaning?

The effect of sleep paralysis episodes has been reported to differ substantially based on a person's cultural background.

Atonia is normally distressing, and scary hallucinations can make episodes even more disturbing. For this reason, around 90% of episodes are related to dread, whilst just a handful have more pleasant or even ecstatic hallucinations.

Episodes can run from a few seconds to 20 minutes, and the average length is around six minutes.

In most cases, episodes terminate on their own but occasionally are interrupted by another person's touch or voice, or by a huge attempt to move that overpowers atonia.

How Common Is Sleep Paralysis?
The prevalence varies, but studies think that around 20% of persons have sleep paralysis at some point throughout their life. There is scant evidence within this group about how often occurrences recur.

Sleep paralysis can occur at any age, but first symptoms often show up in childhood, adolescence, or young adulthood. After starting throughout teenage years, episodes may occur more regularly throughout a person's 20s and 30s.

CAUSES OF SLEEP PARALYSIS
Sleep paralysis is an intriguing and confusing sleep disorder that has captivated

and baffled scientists, researchers, and individuals alike.

The causes of sleep paralysis comprise a complex interplay of neurophysiological, psychological, and cultural elements. In this comprehensive analysis, we examine the multiple explanations and contributing aspects that explain sleep paralysis occurrences, shedding light on the cryptic nature of this intriguing occurrence.

Disruption of Sleep-Wake Transitions

One of the major causes of sleep paralysis resides in the interruption of regular sleep-wake transitions. During sleep, the brain undergoes numerous stages of sleep, including non-rapid eye movement (NREM) sleep and rapid eye movement (REM) sleep.

Sleep paralysis occurs during the transition between distinct sleep stages, notably during the transition from REM sleep to waking (hypnopompic sleep paralysis) or the transition from awake to REM sleep (hypnagogic sleep paralysis).

REM Sleep and Muscle Paralysis

REM sleep is characterised by strong brain activity and vivid dreams. To safeguard individuals from acting out their dreams and perhaps injuring themselves during REM sleep, the brain generates muscle paralysis, known as REM atonia.

In sleep paralysis, this muscle paralysis continues even after the subject regains awareness, leading to the inability to move or talk.

Sleep Deprivation and Irregular Sleep Patterns

Lack of appropriate sleep and irregular sleep cycles can increase the chance of sleep paralysis. Sleep deprivation can alter regular sleep cycles and increase the frequency of REM sleep, resulting in a higher occurrence of sleep paralysis episodes. Irregular sleep patterns, such as shift work or jet lag, can also affect the typical sleep-wake transitions and contribute to sleep paralysis.

Narcolepsy and Other Sleep Disorders
Sleep paralysis is intimately associated with narcolepsy, a neurological sleep condition characterised by excessive daytime sleepiness and sudden sleep bouts.

Individuals with narcolepsy commonly experience sleep paralysis as a symptom of their disease due to the abnormalities in their sleep-wake cycles.

Additionally, sleep paralysis can co-occur with other sleep disorders, such as sleep apnea or insomnia, further complicating the sleep architecture and contributing to sleep paralysis episodes.

Stress & Anxiety
Psychological factors, such as stress and anxiety, can trigger or intensify sleep

paralysis episodes. High amounts of stress and concern can affect sleep patterns and lead to fragmented sleep, increasing the likelihood of developing sleep paralysis.

Furthermore, fear and anxiety linked with earlier sleep paralysis episodes can produce a cycle of anticipatory anxiety, making future bouts more likely.

<u>Sleep Disorders Related to REM Sleep</u>
Apart from narcolepsy, several sleep disorders related to REM sleep could be associated with sleep paralysis. For instance, REM sleep behaviour disorder (RBD), in which individuals act out their dreams during REM sleep due to a lack of muscle paralysis, can contribute to the sense of sleep paralysis as the brain struggles to transition smoothly between REM sleep and waking.

Familial and Genetic Factors

Some study suggests that sleep paralysis may have a familial or genetic component, with an increased probability of developing sleep paralysis if close family members have a history of the illness. However, greater research is needed to thoroughly understand the genetic origins of sleep paralysis.

Cultural and Social Influences

Cultural beliefs and superstitions involving sleep paralysis can alter individuals' perceptions and interpretations of the experiences. In various cultures, sleep paralysis is associated with supernatural creatures or spirits, leading to heightened fear and anxiety during episodes. Cultural views may also influence the probability of reporting sleep paralysis incidents and getting treatment.

<u>Sleep Disorders and Medications</u>

Certain medicines, such as those used to treat insomnia or mental issues, may disturb sleep patterns and contribute to sleep paralysis. Moreover, medicines that change REM sleep, such as antidepressants, can influence the occurrence of sleep paralysis episodes.

The causes of sleep paralysis comprise a complex interplay of neurophysiological, psychological, and cultural elements. From problems in sleep-wake transitions and REM sleep muscle paralysis to psychological strain and worry, various factors could contribute to the prevalence of sleep paralysis episodes.

Additionally, sleep disorders such narcolepsy and REM sleep behaviour disorder may be directly connected with sleep paralysis occurrences.

Understanding the causes of sleep paralysis is vital in providing effective care and treatment for those affected by this strange sleep illness.

As research continues to unearth the complexity of sleep paralysis, our understanding of the underlying mechanisms and contributing factors will increase, paving the way for more effective therapy and care for those suffering this unique phenomena.

SLEEP DISORDERS

Sleep disorders and other sleeping disturbances have exhibited some of the greatest connections with isolated sleep paralysis. Higher rates of sleep paralysis — 38% in one research study -- are observed by people with obstructive sleep apnea (OSA), a sleep disorder marked by frequent disruptions in breathing.

Sleep paralysis also has been reported to be more common in persons with persistent insomnia, circadian rhythm disruption, and nighttime leg cramps.

Narcolepsy

A pattern of multiple instances of sleep paralysis over some period may be connected with narcolepsy. Narcolepsy can impair the function of neurotransmitters in the brain, which may generate complications during REM sleep, including sleep paralysis.

While roughly 20% of the general population has intermittent bouts of sleep paralysis, episodes are generally more common in those with narcolepsy. Consider consulting with your doctor if you observe indications of narcolepsy, including episodes of falling asleep without warning at inappropriate times, extreme daytime tiredness, or muscle weakness.

Mental Health Disorders

Certain mental health conditions have revealed an association to sleep paralysis. Some of the greatest associations are among persons with post-traumatic stress disorder (PTSD) and others who have been exposed to physical and mental pain.

Those with anxiety disorders, particularly panic disorder, also appear to be more prone to have the condition. Stopping alcohol or antidepressants could lead to REM rebound, which may potentially trigger sleep paralysis.

Studies have demonstrated an elevated risk in those with a family history of sleep paralysis, but no precise genetic foundation has been uncovered.

Dream Patterns

Some research has found that persons who demonstrate features of imaginativeness and disassociation from their immediate environment, such as daydreaming, are more prone to sleep paralysis. There may be a link as well between sleep paralysis and vivid nightmares or lucid dreaming. Further research is necessary to investigate these linkages and better understand the numerous potential causes of sleep paralysis.

Is Sleep Paralysis Dangerous?
For most people, sleep paralysis is not considered hazardous. Though it may induce mental anguish, it is viewed as a benign ailment and normally does not arise frequently enough to produce severe health implications.

However, an estimated 10% of persons endure more recurring or unpleasant episodes that make sleep paralysis particularly problematic.

As a result, people may acquire unfavourable views about going to bed, limiting the time given for sleep, or producing anxiety around bedtime that makes it harder to obtain deep sleep. This resultant sleep loss can lead to excessive daytime sleepiness and many harmful effects for a person's general health.

TYPES OF SLEEP PARALYSIS

Sleep paralysis is a sleep disorder characterised by a momentary incapacity to move or speak during falling asleep or waking up. There are fundamentally two varieties of sleep paralysis:

1. <u>Hypnagogic Sleep Paralysis:</u> This form of sleep paralysis occurs when a person encounters the condition while falling asleep. It commonly happens during the transition between awake and sleep, in the "hypnagogic" state. People may have strong hallucinations and a sensation of approaching danger during this form of sleep paralysis.

2. <u>Hypnopompic Sleep Paralysis:</u> This type of sleep paralysis occurs when a person experiences the condition when waking up from sleep. It occurs during the transition from sleep to waking, in the "hypnopompic" condition. Similar to hypnagogic sleep paralysis, individuals may also have hallucinations and sentiments of terror or dread.

Both hypnagogic and hypnopompic sleep paralysis episodes can be exceedingly distressing, as the victim is aware of their surroundings yet unable to move or talk. These episodes generally last for a few seconds to a few minutes but could feel much longer to the individual experiencing them.

Sleep paralysis can be related with numerous conditions, including sleep deprivation, irregular sleep schedule, narcolepsy, stress, anxiety, and specific sleep disorders.

While it could be a scary experience, it is generally not judged hazardous on its own. However, underlying sleep difficulties or other medical conditions should be investigated and treated by a healthcare practitioner if sleep paralysis becomes regular or adversely damages one's well-being.

THE CONNECTION BETWEEN SLEEP PARALYSIS AND LUCID DREAMING

It's worth mentioning that some folks with an interest in lucid dreaming may use sleep paralysis as a stepping stone to enter a lucid dream. Lucid dreaming is when the dreamer becomes aware that they are dreaming and can exert some level of control over the dream's content.

During sleep paralysis, the mind is in a unique situation, and with effort, some individuals can move from the paralyzed state to a lucid dream by adopting specialised tactics, like visualisation and intention-setting.

Sleep paralysis is a strange and frequently terrifying sleep disorder distinguished by temporary paralysis and vivid hallucinations. Although it is frequently not hazardous on its own, it can be an alarming experience for those who encounter it.

Understanding the signs of sleep paralysis can help individuals recognize and cope with these episodes while obtaining professional help may be important for those whose sleep paralysis becomes regular or seriously disrupts their everyday lives.

As research continues to shed light on the mechanics behind this mysterious occurrence, the knowledge and therapy of sleep paralysis are likely to improve, bringing reprieve to those affected by this unsettling state.

SLEEP PARALYSIS AND CO-OCCURRING CONDITIONS

Sleep paralysis, a fascinating and scary phenomenon, is often not a unique experience. It can co-occur with multiple sleep disorders and mental health difficulties, causing a dynamic interplay that affects an individual's well-being and overall sleep quality.

In this part, we will explore deeper into the relationship between sleep paralysis and co-occurring disorders, giving insight into their intertwined nature and potential repercussions for persons affected.

Co-occurrence with Sleep Disorders

a. Narcolepsy: Narcolepsy is a neurological condition characterised by excessive daytime sleepiness, unexpected and uncontrollable bouts of sleep (known as "sleep attacks"), and anomalies in the sleep-wake cycle.

Sleep paralysis is a typical symptom of narcolepsy, often occurring as patients transition between wakefulness and sleep. It is a result of the fast entry into REM sleep, causing brief paralysis while the person is still conscious.

b. <u>REM Sleep Behavior condition (RBD):</u> RBD is a sleep condition in which individuals physically play out their dreams during REM sleep, often due to the absence of the normal muscle paralysis that accompanies REM sleep. In some cases, sleep paralysis can arise as a result of the transition between REM sleep and awareness in patients with RBD.

c. <u>Sleep Apnea:</u> Sleep apnea is defined as disrupted breathing during sleep, resulting in brief awakenings throughout the night. Sleep apnea can contribute to disturbed sleep patterns and may increase the probability of developing sleep paralysis.

d.   <u>Sleep-related Panic Attacks</u>: Some patients may experience panic attacks during sleep or upon waking, leading to a heightened level of worry and a higher risk of sleep paralysis episodes.

<u>Co-occurrence with Mental Health Conditions</u>

a. <u>Anxiety Disorders</u>: Anxiety disorders, such as generalised anxiety disorder and panic disorder, are typically related with sleep issues, including sleep paralysis. High levels of stress and concern can affect sleep patterns and contribute to the incidence of sleep paralysis episodes.

b. <u>Post-Traumatic Stress Disorder (PTSD)</u>: PTSD can contribute to sleep disorders, nightmares, and abnormalities in sleep architecture. Sleep paralysis may be more likely in persons with PTSD due to the influence of trauma on sleep.

c. <u>Depression:</u> Depression is generally associated with sleep difficulties, including insomnia and disturbed sleep cycles. Sleep paralysis may be more likely in persons with depression.

Sleep Deprivation and Irregular Sleep Patterns

Sleep deprivation and irregular sleep cycles are substantial risk factors for both sleep paralysis and numerous sleep disorders. People with irregular sleep habits or severe sleep deprivation may be more prone to encounter sleep paralysis episodes.

Reciprocal Relationship

The link between sleep paralysis and co-occurring illnesses is often bidirectional. Sleep problems and mental health concerns can contribute to sleep interruptions and, in turn, increase the probability of developing sleep paralysis. Conversely, sleep paralysis can lead to heightened concern, terror, and sleep interruptions, aggravating underlying mental health issues.

Sleep paralysis and co-occurring disorders create a tangled web that intertwines sleep difficulties, mental health, and overall well-being. Understanding the links between sleep paralysis and sleep disorders, as well as mental health difficulties, is crucial for designing effective treatments and treatment strategies.

Differentiating Sleep Paralysis from Other Sleep Disorders

Sleep disorders involve a vast array of illnesses that interrupt regular sleep patterns and impact millions of individuals worldwide. Among these illnesses, sleep paralysis stands out as a distinct and unusual phenomenon.

In this lengthy examination, we delve into the particular features of sleep paralysis, comparing and contrasting it with other sleep disorders to better grasp its characteristics and ramifications.

1. Sleep Paralysis:

Definition: Sleep paralysis is a sleep condition characterised by transient muscle paralysis, generally occurring during the transition between wakefulness and sleep (hypnagogic) or when waking up (hypnopompic). During these episodes, individuals are alert and aware of their surroundings but unable to move or talk.

Key Features:

- Temporary paralysis of voluntary muscles during waking or sleep transitions.
- Vivid hallucinations often accompany the events.
- Intense feelings, such as fear or worry, are typical during the encounter.
- Sleep paralysis can be single episodes or part of a broader sleep problem like narcolepsy.

2. Narcolepsy:

Definition: Narcolepsy is a chronic neurological disorder distinguished by severe daytime sleepiness, sudden and unpredictable sleep attacks, and anomalies in the sleep-wake cycle.

Key Features:
- Excessive daytime sleepiness, which can lead to unexpected and involuntary periods of sleep.
- Cataplexy, an abrupt loss of muscle tone triggered by intense emotions, often laughing or enthusiasm.
- Sleep paralysis can be a prominent symptom of narcolepsy, occurring as patients move into or out of REM sleep.

3. REM Sleep Behavior Disorder (RBD):

Definition: REM Sleep Behavior Disorder is a sleep disorder in which individuals physically act out their dreams during REM sleep, potentially inflicting injury to themselves or others.

Key Features:
- Acting out dreams during REM sleep due to the absence of usual muscle paralysis.
- RBD involves motions, such as kicking, punching, or talking during sleep.
- Unlike sleep paralysis, RBD does not involve the experience of temporary paralysis while being awake and aware.

4. Insomnia:
Definition: Insomnia is a sleep condition characterised by difficulties getting asleep, staying asleep, or waking up too early and struggling to fall back asleep.

Key Features:
- Persistent difficulty with sleep initiation or maintenance, leading to sleep deprivation.

- Sleep paralysis is not a typical symptom of insomnia unless it arises during sleep-wake transitions.

5. Sleep Apnea:

Definition: Sleep apnea is a sleep disorder characterised by pauses in breathing during sleep, resulting in brief awakenings and changes in sleep patterns.

Key Features:

- Frequent disturbances in breathing during sleep, generating snoring and daytime weariness.
- Sleep apnea can lead to sleep interruptions, although it does not entail the brief paralysis encountered in sleep paralysis.

6. Restless Legs Syndrome (RLS):

Definition: Restless Legs Syndrome is a neurological disorder characterised by uncomfortable sensations in the legs, often leading to an irresistible need to move them.

Key Features:
- Sensations of pain, tingling, or crawling in the legs, often alleviated by movement.
- RLS can disrupt sleep patterns, however it does not entail the temporary paralysis encountered in sleep paralysis.

7. Exploding Head Syndrome (EHS):
Definition: Exploding Head Syndrome is a sleep disorder characterised by the perception of loud noises, such as explosions or crashes, during the transition between alertness and sleep.

Key Features:
- Auditory hallucinations of loud noises that seem to originate from within the head.
- EHS is separate from sleep paralysis, which involves brief paralysis and often visual or tactile hallucinations.

While sleep disorders span a vast spectrum of ailments, sleep paralysis remains a distinct and intriguing event. Its unique features, such as temporary muscle paralysis, vivid hallucinations, and conscious awareness throughout the episodes, distinguish it from other sleep disorders.

Understanding the traits that separate sleep paralysis from other sleep-related diseases is crucial for proper diagnosis and appropriate management.

By unravelling the precise threads of sleep paralysis, we acquire valuable insights into the intricacy of the human mind and the confusing nature of sleep disorders.

Chapter 2

SLEEP PARALYSIS IN DIFFERENT CULTURES AND HISTORICAL CONTEXTS

Sleep paralysis, with its peculiar properties of transitory muscle paralysis and vivid hallucinations, has attracted the attention and imagination of societies worldwide throughout history.

Across numerous cultures and historical times, sleep paralysis has been viewed through various lenses, including spiritual, mystical, and supernatural perspectives.

In this chapter, we examine the unique forms of sleep paralysis in different cultures and its relevance in historical contexts, bringing insight into the spectrum of beliefs and interpretations surrounding this mysterious sleep phenomenon.

Sleep Paralysis in Ancient Cultures

In ancient civilizations, sleep paralysis was commonly associated with the power of gods, spirits, or supernatural forces. For example, in ancient Greece, sleep paralysis was associated with the figure of "Morpheus," the deity of dreams.

The term "nightmare" originates from the Old English word "mare," referring to a horrible spirit thought to cause suffocation during sleep, which closely matches sleep paralysis events.

Ancient Egyptian mythology also included monsters called "demons" or "night hags" believed to produce sleep disorders, including sleep paralysis.

In many ancient communities, individuals undergoing sleep paralysis episodes were thought to be in a position of vulnerability, rendering them susceptible to contacts with the spirit realm.

<u>Sleep Paralysis in Middle Ages and Renaissance</u>

During the Middle Ages and the Renaissance, beliefs in witches, devils, and malicious spirits altered the interpretation of sleep paralysis incidents. Reports of nightly visitations by witches and demonic creatures were frequent, and sleep paralysis episodes were generally associated with such experiences.

The pervasive fear of supernatural entities led to the notion that sleep paralysis was proof of being possessed or haunted by bad spirits.

In literature and art from this period, sleep paralysis and accompanying occurrences were depicted in vivid and often horrific imagery, thus bolstering society views about the spiritual and malicious components of sleep paralysis.

Sleep Paralysis in Asian Cultures

In many Asian cultures, sleep paralysis has been related to folklore and spiritual beliefs. For instance, in Japan, sleep paralysis is referred to as "kanashibari" and is supposed to be caused by malevolent spirits or ghosts.

The phrase "kanashibari" translates to "bound by metal" or "bound by iron," characterising the sensation of physical confinement experienced during sleep paralysis.

In Thai folklore, sleep paralysis is known as "phi am" and is associated with the presence of an evil spirit or ghost sitting on the chest of the sleeping person, resulting in the sense of suffocation.

Sleep Paralysis in African and Caribbean Cultures

In some African and Caribbean cultures, sleep paralysis is sometimes understood through the lens of "witchcraft" or "voodoo." Individuals suffering sleep paralysis may attribute their episodes to the destructive activities of witches or practitioners of black magic.

Beliefs in curses, hexes, and supernatural powers have a vital influence in defining interpretations of sleep paralysis incidents in diverse cultural contexts.

Sleep Paralysis in Modern Cultures

In present times, while scientific reasons for sleep paralysis are accessible, cultural beliefs and interpretations still influence individuals' experiences and views of this occurrence.

In various cultures, sleep paralysis continues to be associated with spiritual encounters, alien abductions, or contact with extraterrestrial species. Pop culture, movies, and literature have also helped to define current ideas of sleep paralysis, generally showing it as a frightening and supernatural experience.

<u>Cultural Practices and Coping Mechanisms</u>

In addition to altering beliefs and perceptions, cultural behaviours and coping techniques connected with sleep paralysis are significant in different communities.

For instance, in some cultures, amulets, talismans, or religious symbols are deployed as protective measures against sleep paralysis and malevolent spirits. Individuals may execute rituals or prayers before sleep to seek protection against sleep disturbances and to ensure peaceful rest.

In other cultures, community support and shared experiences play a vital part in coping with sleep paralysis. Communities may band together to share tales and give support, fostering a sense of kinship and solidarity among persons who have sleep paralysis. This collective understanding and support might be effective in alleviating the fear and anxiety associated with sleep paralysis episodes.

Influence of Art, Literature, and Media

Throughout history and across cultures, sleep paralysis has been a recurring motif in art, literature, and mythology. Paintings, sculptures, and literary works have depicted night terrors, incubi, and other indicators of sleep paralysis. These visuals usually mirror current cultural views and superstitions about the supernatural and the spirit realm.

In the contemporary age, media, including films, television shows, and internet content, have continued to represent sleep paralysis in various ways, typically sensationalising and dramatising the experiences.

Such visuals can alter public perceptions toward sleep paralysis, disseminating myths and contributing to emotions of fear and worry among persons who experience it.

The Globalization of Sleep Paralysis Experiences

With the rise of worldwide communication and the internet, sleep paralysis experiences from many cultures are now more accessible to a global audience.

Online forums and social media platforms enable individuals from diverse cultural backgrounds to share their sleep paralysis experiences and interpretations. This globalisation of sleep paralysis experiences gives for a broader awareness of the phenomena and highlights the linkages and contrasts in cultural interpretations.

Scientific Perspectives and Cultural Sensitivity

While cultural beliefs and interpretations of sleep paralysis are vital to understanding its significance in different societies, it is crucial to approach the topic with cultural awareness and respect.

Scientific opinions on sleep paralysis, grounded in neurophysiology and psychology, offer essential insights into the mechanisms driving this sleep disorder.

Balancing scientific knowledge with cultural understanding is crucial in providing complete care for patients experiencing sleep paralysis.

Healthcare professionals and researchers need to acknowledge and respect cultural beliefs while giving evidence-based explanations and aid for affected persons.

The Future of Cultural Perspectives on Sleep Paralysis

As cultures grow and interact in a more interconnected globe, cultural attitudes toward sleep paralysis may continue to shift. Cultural influences on sleep paralysis episodes can adapt and vary with time, influenced by factors such as education, urbanisation, and globalisation.

The integration of scientific knowledge and cultural perspectives in research and healthcare can lead to more holistic techniques of understanding and regulating sleep paralysis.

By recognizing the significance of cultural concepts and experiences, researchers and healthcare practitioners can design culturally sensitive interventions and support systems adapted to the unique requirements of individuals and communities.

Sleep paralysis has maintained an essential position in the beliefs, mythology, and cultural traditions of many nations throughout history. From ancient civilizations to modern globalised communities, ideas of sleep paralysis have been shaped by spiritual beliefs, mythology, and supernatural perceptions.

Cultural traditions and coping mechanisms linked with sleep paralysis reveal the ways in which communities come together to address and make sense of this unique event.

While scientific research offers important insights into the neurophysiological components of sleep paralysis, cultural opinions remain an integral aspect of the human experience.

Combining scientific expertise with cultural sensitivity is crucial in providing thorough treatment and support for patients experiencing sleep paralysis, ensuring that various beliefs and interpretations are recognized and integrated into healthcare practices.

As civilizations continue to grow, so too will the cultural perspectives on sleep paralysis, enhancing our awareness of this enigmatic and interesting sleep event.

Chapter 3

<u>LUCID DREAMING</u>

Lucid dreaming is a fascinating and absorbing experience that allows individuals to become aware that they are dreaming while the dream is still occurring. In this level of heightened consciousness, lucid dreamers have the astounding ability to identify that they are in a dream world, separate from their waking reality.

With this awareness, they can actively participate in and affect the dream narrative, leading to thrilling and altering dream experiences. In this extensive analysis, we dig into the definition and explanation of lucid dreaming, finding the physics behind this astounding occurrence and its prospective repercussions for our knowledge of consciousness.

Definition of Lucid Dreaming

Lucid dreaming can be defined as a condition of dreaming in which the dreamer is aware that they are dreaming, maintaining a sense of consciousness and self-awareness inside the dream environment.

This heightened level of consciousness helps individuals to perceive the distinction between the dream world and waking reality, enabling them to engage with and impact the dream narrative to some extent.

Characteristics of Lucid Dreaming

1. <u>Conscious Awareness:</u> The main aspect of lucid dreaming is the dreamer's conscious awareness of the dream experience. Lucid dreamers know that they are dreaming while the dream is still unfolding, which identifies this sort of dream as unique from usual dreaming experiences.

2. <u>Control over Actions:</u> In lucid dreams, individuals may have various degrees of control over their actions and the dream environment. They can make decisions, influence the dream's trajectory, or interact with dream characters and elements consciously.

3. <u>Reality Testing:</u> Lucid dreamers often utilise reality testing techniques to confirm their lucid condition. These strategies involve monitoring the dream environment for discrepancies, trying to study literature or gaze at a clock (which may vary or appear distorted in dreams), or doing physical feats, including flying or passing through walls.

4. <u>Emotional Experience:</u> Lucid dreaming can generate immense sensations, ranging from elation and astonishment to terror and wonder. The emotional intensity of lucid dreams can be heightened by the dreamer's awareness of the dream's deceptive quality.

THE SCIENCE BEHIND LUCID DREAMING

The phenomena of lucid dreaming have been a topic of scientific investigation for decades. While the particular mechanisms supporting lucid dreaming are not entirely understood, numerous ideas and findings provide insight into its probable neurophysiological basis:

1. Activation of the Prefrontal Cortex: The prefrontal cortex, responsible for higher-order cognitive tasks, including decision-making and self-awareness, plays a critical role in lucid dreaming. Studies utilising electroencephalography (EEG) have indicated greater activity in the prefrontal cortex during lucid dreams, suggesting that this brain region may be implicated in the state of self-awareness.

2. REM Sleep and Dreaming: Lucid dreaming is most frequently reported to occur during Rapid Eye Movement (REM)

sleep, a sleep condition related to vivid dreams. During REM sleep, the brain is extraordinarily active, similar to waking consciousness. The heightened activity in the brain during REM sleep may enhance conscious awareness within dreams.

3. <u>Gamma Band Activity:</u> Some studies have discovered greater gamma band activity in the brain during lucid dreaming. Gamma oscillations are related with heightened cognitive processing and are believed to be involved in conscious consciousness.

4. <u>Dopaminergic System:</u> The neurotransmitter dopamine has been engaged in the regulation of lucid dreaming. Changes in dopamine levels or the sensitivity of dopamine receptors may influence the likelihood of experiencing lucid dreams.

Potential Applications and Implications of Lucid Dreaming

The exploration of lucid dreaming extends beyond its fascinating character, suggesting potential applications and ramifications in several fields:

1. <u>Therapeutic Use:</u> Lucid dreaming has been explored as a potential therapeutic tool for managing nightmares, trauma, and anxiety-related problems. The capacity to face and change dream content in a conscious state may deliver therapeutic benefits to those struggling with frequent nightmares or painful experiences.

2. <u>Creativity and Problem-Solving:</u> Some academics suggest that lucid dreaming may increase creativity and problem-solving skills. Lucid dreamers can actively explore creative ideas, model scenarios, and experiment with solutions in the safe environment of dreams.

3. <u>Spiritual and Transcendental Experiences:</u> For select individuals, lucid

dreaming may offer potential for spiritual discovery and experiences of transcendence. Lucid dreams have been related to mystical states, giving a unique vision of awareness and reality.

Lucid dreaming is a captivating and engaging experience that unlocks the realm of conscious awareness within the world of dreams. With the ability to notice and engage with the dream environment, lucid dreamers navigate a unique and transformative level of consciousness.

While the scientific understanding of lucid dreaming continues to develop, research suggests that neuronal activity in the prefrontal cortex, REM sleep, gamma band activity, and the dopaminergic system may play a role in enabling lucid dreams.

Beyond its intriguing aspect, lucid dreaming provides potential benefits in therapeutic settings and artistic study. The study of lucid dreaming offers essential insights into the complexity of awareness during sleep and creates routes for further exploration into the enigmatic realm of dreams.

As the study proceeds, the phenomena of lucid dreaming may continue to disclose new chances for studying the human mind and its link with the enigmatic world of sleep.

The Intriguing Relationship Between Sleep Paralysis and Lucid Dreams

The link between sleep paralysis and lucid dreams is an intriguing and complex one, as both phenomena require unique states of awareness that occur during sleep.

On one side, lucid dreaming empowers individuals with conscious awareness and control within dreams, allowing them to actively influence their dream experiences. On the other side, sleep paralysis creates a sharp contrast, with transient muscle paralysis and intense hallucinations, leaving patients briefly immobile and often experiencing panic and helplessness.

In this extensive section, we delve into the complexities of the relationship between sleep paralysis and lucid dreams, uncovering their different qualities, probable connections, and repercussions for our understanding of the human mind during sleep.

Understanding Lucid Dreams and Sleep Paralysis

a. Lucid Dreams: Lucid dreams are defined by the dreamer's awareness that they are dreaming while the dream is still unfolding. In lucid dreams, individuals maintain consciousness and self-awareness within the dream world, enabling them to actively participate in and even influence the dream narrative.

b. <u>Sleep Paralysis:</u> Sleep paralysis is a sleep condition that involves brief muscle paralysis during the transition between wakefulness and sleep (hypnagogic) or upon waking up (hypnopompic). In these episodes, individuals are alert and aware of their surroundings but unable to move or talk.

Lucid Dreaming as an Escape from Sleep Paralysis

For individuals who have recurring episodes of sleep paralysis, lucid dreaming can give a potential escape from distressing situations. By mastering the method of lucid dreaming, these individuals may be able to recognize the onset of sleep paralysis inside a dream and turn the experience into a lucid dream.

In this lucid state, people may gain control over their dream activities and the dream environment, allowing them to alter the narrative away from fear-inducing hallucinations.

<u>Sleep Paralysis During Lucid Dreams</u>

Conversely, in rare instances, lucid dreamers may face sleep paralysis-like emotions within their lucid dreams. This scenario could be disturbing, since the dreamer may be aware of their lucid status but still have the physical sensation of being briefly immobilised.

However, in a lucid dream, the dreamer is more likely to approach sleep paralysis symptoms with a sense of inquiry and detachment, knowing that it is a transitory dream experience.

<u>The Wake-Induced Lucid Dream (WILD) Technique</u>

The Wake-Induced Lucid Dream (WILD) technique is a method used to induce lucid dreams instantly from awake. During this method, individuals maintain consciousness while moving from a wakeful state to a lucid dream state.

The WILD approach may involve experiencing sensations comparable to sleep paralysis, such as physiological paralysis and auditory or visual hallucinations. Mastering the WILD technique needs a precise balance of preserving awareness while navigating the dream-entering process.

The Emotional Impact

The emotional experiences of lucid dreaming and sleep paralysis could dramatically differ. Lucid dreaming is typically related with feelings of empowerment, excitement, and wonder, as individuals embrace the ability to explore and affect their dream experiences.

In contrast, sleep paralysis is renowned for its painful aspect, with feelings of worry, helplessness, and vulnerability, especially when accompanied by vivid and frequently frightening hallucinations.

The Boundary Between Consciousness and Sleep

The link between sleep paralysis and lucid dreams demonstrates the interesting and sometimes delicate border between consciousness and sleep.

Both experiences challenge our awareness of the bounds of consciousness during sleep and raise problems regarding the inner workings of the human mind during these confusing states.

Implications for Understanding Consciousness

The study of the relationship between sleep paralysis and lucid dreams offers significant insights into the complexity of consciousness during sleep. The ability to preserve self-awareness and control within dreams challenges typical ideas of consciousness and demonstrates that consciousness may be more flexible and dynamic during sleep than previously assumed.

Practical Applications and Therapeutic Potential

Understanding the relationship between sleep paralysis and lucid dreams may have practical advantages, particularly in therapeutic contexts. For those who have terrible sleep paralysis episodes, acquiring lucid dreaming abilities can potentially give a coping mechanism and a means to turn traumatic occurrences into more positive and empowering dream narratives.

The intriguing relationship between sleep paralysis and lucid dreams is a fascinating exploration of the small line between control and paralysis within the domain of sleep.

Lucid dreaming empowers individuals with conscious awareness and agency in their dream experiences, but sleep paralysis confronts them with momentary muscle paralysis and vivid hallucinations.

For some individuals, lucid dreaming offers a potential escape from the distress of sleep paralysis, while for others, sleep paralysis feelings may occasionally occur inside their lucid dreams. The analysis of this relationship raises problems concerning the complexity of consciousness during sleep and the capacity for awareness to adapt and evolve during distinct sleep stages.

A study in the disciplines of sleep and consciousness continues, and further insights may be gleaned into the confusing link between sleep paralysis and lucid dreams. Ultimately, knowing these distinct experiences can expand our understanding of the human mind during sleep and provide practical applications for coping with and navigating the complexities of the dream world.

Chapter 4

HISTORICAL AND CULTURAL PERSPECTIVES ON SLEEP PARALYSIS

Sleep paralysis is a fascinating and terrible phenomenon that has caught the curiosity of different cultures throughout history.

With roots in ancient folklore, religious beliefs, and superstitions, sleep paralysis has been studied and described via numerous cultural lenses. Let's analyse the historical and cultural opinions on sleep paralysis, following its history from mystical interpretations to present scientific understanding.

Ancient and Folkloric Interpretations

In many ancient civilizations, sleep paralysis was often attributed to supernatural or paranormal animals. Across cultures, these phenomena were identified with evil spirits, demons, ghosts, or terrible monsters.

The experiences of sleep paralysis were supposed to be in communication with these otherworldly beings, and interpretations differed depending on cultural context and local beliefs.

For example:
In Scandinavian legend, "mara" or "mare" was a wicked monster that perched on a person's chest during sleep, inflicting paralysis and suffocation. This concept possibly gave rise to the English phrase "nightmare."

In Japanese legend, "kanashibari" alluded to a similar situation where a ghost or spirit would pin a person down, leading to sleep paralysis.

In African and Afro-Caribbean cultures, sleep paralysis was commonly associated with malevolent spirits like the "Old Hag" or "Soucouyant," believed to produce sleep disorders and paralysis.

Religious and Supernatural Beliefs

In many religious traditions, sleep paralysis was regarded as a manifestation of supernatural forces in action. It was often understood through the lens of religious ideals and the fight between good and evil.

- In some Christian contexts, sleep paralysis was associated with demonic possession or the presence of malevolent spirits. The incapacity to move or talk was attributed to the oppression of dark forces.

- In Islamic traditions, sleep paralysis was associated with "Jinn," otherworldly beings fashioned from smokeless fire, said to interact with humans during sleep and dreams.

<u>Cultural Influence on Hallucinations</u>

The appearance of vivid hallucinations during sleep paralysis has also been altered by cultural beliefs and legends. The substance of these hallucinations often parallels the mythology and supernatural entities particular to each culture.

- For instance, folks in Western cultures could perceive dark entities like ghosts or demons, reflecting the preponderance of such imagery in their folklore.

- In non-Western cultures, the hallucinations may take the form of culturally specific beings, such as spirits or legendary creatures.

<u>Sleep Paralysis Art and Literature</u>

Sleep paralysis has also left its mark on art, literature, and other sorts of creative expression. Famous artworks, poetry, and novels have expressed the uncanny sensations of sleep paralysis, reflecting cultural ideals and psychological views.

- Henry Fuseli's image "The Nightmare" (1781) is a classic example, portraying a woman lying in bed with an incubus on her chest, believed to indicate sleep paralysis.

- Edgar Allan Poe's short story "The Fall of the House of Usher" (1839) features a character undergoing sleep paralysis amid an unsettling and gloomy milieu.

Shift Towards Scientific Understanding

As scientific knowledge expanded and our understanding of sleep and dreams improved, the interpretation of sleep paralysis shifted away from supernatural explanations to more rational and medical perspectives.

- In the late 19th and early 20th centuries, sleep researchers and psychologists began to examine sleep paralysis as a sleep-related condition, relating it to REM sleep and the transient loss of muscle tone when dreaming.

- Today, sleep paralysis is recognized as a sleep disorder that can develop owing to irregularities in the sleep-wake cycle, sleep deprivation, irregular sleep patterns, narcolepsy, and other reasons.

Contemporary Cultural Influence

Despite the shift towards scientific understanding, traditional beliefs, and folklore still impact how some individuals perceive and interpret their sleep paralysis experiences. Cultural background can alter the feelings, sensations, and entities encountered during sleep paralysis episodes.

Cultural Variations and Contemporary Interpretations

One remarkable component of cultural perspectives on sleep paralysis is the wide difference in the entities and experiences recounted by folks from diverse cultural backgrounds. While some cultures have tales of harmful spirits causing sleep paralysis, others have pleasant or neutral beings supposed to interact with humans during comparable events.

For example:

- In Mexican and Latin American tradition, the "Santo Pelo" (Holy Hair) is regarded as a protecting presence during sleep paralysis, believed to hinder wicked spirits from causing harm.

- In Thai tradition, sleep paralysis is usually associated with encounters with a "Phi Am," a benign spirit or ancestor said to watch over the person during sleep.

- Among the Inuit people of the Arctic, sleep paralysis experiences have been attributed to communication with a creature known as the "Ucu" or "Ijiraq," which may reflect an individual's unsolved problems or past traumas.

These discrepancies mirror the varied belief systems and mythologies of different cultures, showing the profoundly embedded impact of cultural heritage on the perception of sleep paralysis occurrences.

Sleep Paralysis in Art and Media

The unsettling and surreal character of sleep paralysis has also affected contemporary art, literature, and popular media. Artists and authors often draw inspiration from this inexplicable occurrence to create engaging and thought-provoking works.

- In the area of horror fiction and cinema, sleep paralysis has been exploited as a plot tactic, weaving its cryptic and horrible features into narratives. Movies and books have examined the psychological anguish of having sleep paralysis and the blurring of barriers between reality and dreams.

- Visual artists have represented sleep paralysis episodes through odd and symbolic pictures, reflecting the emotion of horror and helplessness associated with these situations.

Cultural Coping Mechanisms

In many cultures, individuals have created coping mechanisms and rituals to protect themselves against sleep paralysis or to mitigate its consequences. These rituals typically require calling protective deities, offering prayers, or deploying talismans to keep off harmful creatures.

Additionally, some cultural norms give collective explanations and social support, helping individuals feel less lonely and distressed by their experiences. Sharing tales of sleep paralysis within cultural contexts could provide a sense of validation and understanding, lowering the fear and stigma associated with these occurrences.

Cultural Implications for Research

Cultural perspectives on sleep paralysis have repercussions for scientific and therapeutic understanding of the phenomenon. In some instances, individuals from specific cultural backgrounds may be more likely to regard sleep paralysis as supernatural or spiritual experiences, forcing them to seek treatment from traditional healers or religious authorities instead of medical doctors.

This cultural background should be acknowledged by academics and clinicians in investigating and treating sleep paralysis. An appreciation of cultural ideas and traditions can allow more effective communication and support for persons experiencing sleep paralysis.

Sleep paralysis continues to be an intriguing and eerie phenomenon that transcends time and cultural borders. The historical and cultural viewpoints on sleep paralysis have shaped how individuals interpret and explain these episodes, ranging from otherworldly encounters to scientific hypotheses based in sleep physiology.

While scientific expertise has shed light on the physiological causes behind sleep paralysis, cultural consequences linger, impacting the perceptions, coping tactics, and communal interpretations of this haunting state.

As the debate between science and culture develops, a holistic understanding of sleep paralysis evolves, incorporating both its neurological basis and its relevance in the cultural fabric of societies worldwide.

With an awareness of the historical and contemporary opinions on sleep paralysis, we acquire deeper insights into the complexities of human experiences and the ongoing fascination of this enigmatic condition.

Chapter 5

<u>SLEEP CYCLE</u>

People don't simply fall asleep and wake up. There are 5 sleep stages we pass through (or should be progressing through) as we nap. It's vital to understand what each of these stages is so we can ensure we're getting into a deep enough slumber. Failure to hit various stages of sleep means biological functions that correlate to that stage aren't happening.

<u>Sleep Stage 1</u>

What it feels like: This stage is easy to experience because it's the stage we come in and out of as we go into sleep. In this stage, a person is readily awoken by the sense of their muscles suddenly clenching or by the sensation of falling. If someone or yourself wakes you from this stage, it may feel like you didn't sleep at all.

What occurs to the body: Blood pressure falls, breathing slows down, heart rate remains steady, and your brain's temperature decreases.

Duration: Stage 1 could last between 1-10 minutes.

Sleep Stage 2

What it feels like: In stage 2 it is tough to rouse someone up as the body begins to settle into profound slumber.

What occurs to the body: Brain waves grow slower with irregular and uncommon bursts of rapid waves. Body temperature starts to fall along with heart rate.

Duration: Sleep Stage 2 takes around 20 minutes to complete, yet we revisit this stage most often as it accounts for about 45% of overall sleep time.

Sleep Stages 3 & 4

What it feels like: Sleep stages 3 and 4 have been combined and are now referred to as the "NREM Stage 3", "slow-wave sleep" or "Delta sleep." In this stage, deep sleep begins. Parasomnias can take place, which include phenomena such as talking in their sleep, sleepwalking, or night terrors.

You will feel nothing in this interval because you will be initialising deep slumber. If you are forced awake you will feel perplexed.

What happens to the body: There are 2 brain waves in this stage of sleep: 1. huge yet slow waves referred to as Delta waves and 2. rapid yet modest waves. The body is immovable, with no eye movement or muscle activity, decreased respiration, and even lower body temperature and blood pressure.

Duration: Between 5-15 minutes.

REM Sleep

What it feels like: Most of your dreams occur during REM. Researchers say that dreams are how the brain absorbs memories, stress, and emotion.

What occurs to the body: Deep sleep is the most restorative sleep state. REM sleep is sometimes called "paradoxical sleep" because brain waves show comparable patterns to a person who is awake.

Duration: REM sleep accounts for around 20% of your entire sleep, but if your cycle is disrupted, the body will demand prolonged periods of REM sleep until you're caught up.

The Importance of Dreams and their Connection to Sleep Paralysis

Dreams have long been a source of wonder and interest for humanity. As we explore the realm of sleep and the mind, we uncover the intricate relationship between dreams and sleep paralysis. In this extensive portion, we dig into the role of dreams and their connection to sleep paralysis, identifying the processes that bind these two confusing phenomena.

1. The Nature of Dreams:

Dreams are a product of the mind's activity during sleep, occurring predominantly during the REM (Rapid Eye Movement) stage of the sleep cycle. While dreaming can occur in other stages as well, REM sleep is characterised by heightened brain activity, vivid mental imagery, and quick eye movements.

During REM sleep, the brain's prefrontal cortex, responsible for rational thinking and decision-making, is less active. This absence of rational control promotes the formation of vivid and oftentimes strange experiences that emerge as dreams.

2. The Connection Between REM Sleep and Sleep Paralysis:

Sleep paralysis is tightly tied to REM sleep and its characteristic qualities. During REM sleep, the brainstem generates neurotransmitters that limit muscular movement, resulting in a state of temporary muscle paralysis known as REM atonia.

This inhibition is necessary to avoid us from physically acting out our dreams and maybe injuring ourselves or others during sleep.

However, in sleep paralysis, this muscle paralysis comes at random moments, leading to the cognitive sense of being unable to move. While the individual's mind is awake and aware, their body remains in a position of immobilisation characteristic of REM sleep.

3. REM Sleep Intrusions:

Sleep paralysis episodes can be considered a form of REM sleep intrusion into consciousness. Instead of transitioning smoothly between sleep stages, the brain temporarily re-enters a REM-like state when the individual is half or awake, resulting in a sense of paralysis.

The introduction of REM sleep components into awareness can potentially account for the vivid hallucinations experienced during sleep paralysis. Aspects of the dreaming state, such as visual and sensory imagery, coupled with the individual's waking vision of reality, resulting in vivid and frequently terrifying hallucinations.

4. Dream Incorporation:

Dream integration is a phenomena in which components of dreams are incorporated into an individual's vision of the waking world. In the case of sleep paralysis, dream integration could show as hallucinations that blend with the individual's actual world.

For example, a person experiencing sleep paralysis may hallucinate the presence of an intruder or a threatening figure in their room, as their dreaming mind combines components of dread and danger with their waking sense of the environment.

5. Lucid Dreaming with Sleep Paralysis:

Lucid dreaming is a state in which the dreamer becomes aware that they are dreaming while the dream is still unfolding. In the context of sleep paralysis, some folks with experience in lucid dreaming techniques may use their awareness to navigate the episode.

By recognizing the state of sleep paralysis as a dream and consciously exerting control over their thoughts and emotions, lucid dreamers can turn the experience into a lucid dream or direct the dream narrative. This ability to exercise some kind of control may alleviate the distress associated with sleep paralysis.

6. Dream Content and Emotional Impact:

Dream content and emotions can greatly alter the sense of sleep paralysis. Stress, anxiety, and other emotional components could affect dream content, hence leading to the existence of threatening or fear-inducing hallucinations during sleep paralysis.

Moreover, the emotional response to sleep paralysis itself can modify the dream content throughout the following episodes. The memory and emotional impact of prior sleep paralysis occurrences may influence the content and severity of hallucinations in subsequent ones.

Dreams and sleep paralysis share a profound and intricate link, both stemming from the complex interaction of the sleeping mind.

As we dive into the area of sleep and dreams, we uncover the mechanisms that give rise to sleep paralysis and its vivid hallucinations. The existence of REM sleep components, dream absorption, and the emotional influence of dream content all intersect to shape the experience of sleep paralysis.

Understanding the relevance of dreams and their connection to sleep paralysis provides us a deeper grasp of the wonders of the human mind during sleep. It also underlines the need of investigating the broader landscape of sleep disorders and mental health to get a complete grasp of sleep paralysis and its influence on persons' lives.

As research improves, we inch closer to discovering the puzzling relationship between dreams and sleep paralysis, shedding light on the delicate workings of

the human mind during the mysterious
condition of sleep.

Chapter 6

DEBUNKING MYTHS ABOUT SLEEP PARALYSIS

Sleep paralysis is an intriguing and sometimes misunderstood phenomenon that has been buried in myths and misconceptions throughout history.

As we seek to obtain a thorough understanding of sleep paralysis, it is vital to dispute these myths and distinguish fact from fiction. In this extensive analysis, we address popular misconceptions regarding sleep paralysis and give evidence-based insights into the true nature of this intriguing sleep illness.

<u>Myth 1: Sleep Paralysis is a Paranormal or Supernatural Phenomenon:</u>

One of the most popular myths regarding sleep paralysis is that it is caused by hostile spirits, demons, or otherworldly beings. Throughout history, sleep paralysis has been linked with mythology and tales of haunting happenings, adding to its reputation as a paranormal occurrence.

Debunked: Sleep paralysis is a well-documented and acknowledged sleep disorder with scientific grounds entrenched in the neurophysiology of sleep. It occurs when there is a momentary detachment between the mind and body during REM sleep or during the transitions between sleep stages.

The hallucinations experienced during sleep paralysis are a consequence of the dreaming mind interacting with awake consciousness, not supernatural powers.

Myth 2: Sleep Paralysis is Harmful or Dangerous:

Due to the unpleasant character of sleep paralysis episodes and the occurrence of vivid hallucinations, many believe that sleep paralysis is harmful and poses a threat to an individual's well-being.

Debunked: Sleep paralysis, on its own, is not physically harmful. While the experience can be painful and emotionally uncomfortable, it does not inflict any physical harm to the body. The transient muscle paralysis during sleep paralysis is a normal protective mechanism that keeps us from acting out our dreams and inflicting injury to ourselves during REM sleep.

Myth 3: Sleep Paralysis is Rare:

Because sleep paralysis is not widely discussed in popular conversations, some feel that it is a unique or rare condition.

Debunked: Sleep paralysis is more widespread than many people realise. Studies suggest that a large percentage of the population experiences sleep paralysis at least once in their lifetime. Estimates vary, but some studies have determined that between 8% to 50% of people have had sleep paralysis at some point.

<u>Myth 4: Sleep Paralysis is Only Experienced During Sleep:</u>

Some individuals may feel that sleep paralysis only occurs throughout the night while sleeping.

Debunked: While sleep paralysis is most typically related with the transition between awake and sleep or while waking up, it can also occur during daytime naps or when individuals have sleep problems owing to irregular sleep-wake patterns.

Myth 5: Sleep Paralysis is a Sign of Mental Illness:

There is a misunderstanding that having sleep paralysis is suggestive of a mental health problem.

Debunked: Sleep paralysis, on its own, is not considered a mental illness. It is a sleep condition that can co-occur with certain mental health issues, but it does not cause mental disease in and of itself.

Myth 6: Sleep Paralysis is Incurable:

Some folks may assume that there is no therapy or solution for sleep paralysis.

Debunked: While there is no one cure for sleep paralysis, identifying its triggers and addressing any co-occurring sleep problems or mental health difficulties will help limit the frequency of episodes. Techniques such as increasing sleep hygiene, keeping a regular sleep schedule, and addressing stress and anxiety can be beneficial in managing sleep paralysis.

Myth 7: Sleep Paralysis Only Happens to People with Sleep Disorders:

There is a misunderstanding that sleep paralysis exclusively affects persons with pre-existing sleep disorders.

Debunked: While sleep disorders like narcolepsy are frequently associated with sleep paralysis, they can also arise in adults without any underlying sleep problem. Sleep paralysis can be triggered by conditions such as sleep deprivation, aberrant sleep cycles, jet lag, and stress.

Myth 8: Sleep Paralysis is Controllable by External Forces:

There is a view among some that external influences, such as supernatural rituals, charms, or spiritual activities, can rule or manipulate sleep paralysis incidents.

Debunked: Sleep paralysis is a neurophysiological phenomena that happens according to the regular functioning of the brain and its sleep-wake mechanisms.

While cultural beliefs and practices may influence how individuals interpret their sleep paralysis experiences, external influences cannot govern or initiate sleep paralysis episodes. The occurrence of sleep paralysis is primarily determined by factors linked to an individual's sleep patterns and sleep-wake cycles.

Myth 9: Everyone Experiences the Same Hallucinations in Sleep Paralysis:

Some may think that the hallucinations experienced during sleep paralysis are uniform and consistent across all individuals.

Debunked: The content of hallucinations during sleep paralysis is quite distinctive and varies widely from person to person. While some folks may report seeing mysterious creatures or menacing objects, others may have totally distinct experiences, such as floating sensations, bright lights, or calm meetings. The content of hallucinations is determined by personal beliefs, cultural background, and individual psychological features.

Myth 10: Sleep Paralysis is Exclusive to Certain Age Groups:

There can be a misunderstanding that sleep paralysis exclusively happens in specific age groups or populations.

Debunked: Sleep paralysis can occur at any age and is not limited to a single group. It has been recorded in children, adolescents, adults, and the elderly. While the frequency of sleep paralysis episodes may vary between age groups, it is not limited to any single population.

Myth 11: Sleep Paralysis is a Sign of a Weak Mind or Weak Character:

Some folks may wrongly conclude that having sleep paralysis is an indication of mental weakness or character defects.

Debunked: Sleep paralysis is a common and involuntary condition that can happen to everyone, regardless of their mental ability or character. It is not a reflection of an individual's personal attributes but rather a byproduct of the natural working of the sleep-wake cycle.

Myth 12: Sleep Paralysis is Induced by Sleeping on Your Back:

There is a popular misconception that resting on one's back increases the likelihood of getting sleep paralysis.

Debunked: While certain research has shown that sleep paralysis may be more frequent when resting on one's back, it is not the solitary explanation responsible for its occurrence.

Sleep paralysis can happen in any sleep position and is impacted by various variables, including irregular sleep cycles, sleep deprivation, and underlying sleep disorders.

Debunking beliefs about sleep paralysis is crucial to encourage a better and more accurate understanding of this intriguing sleep illness. By addressing myths and delivering evidence-based information, we may overcome fear, stigma, and misunderstanding linked to sleep paralysis.

Recognizing the scientific origins of sleep paralysis allows us to appreciate the complexity of the human brain and the numerous domains of sleep disorders.

Increased understanding and education surrounding sleep paralysis allow individuals to approach their experiences with a sense of knowledge and agency, leading to improved support and management for those affected by this perplexing phenomenon.

Chapter 7

IMPACTS OF SLEEP PARALYSIS

Sleep paralysis is a unique and terrible sleep disorder that can have considerable implications on an individual's life. From psychological and emotional repercussions to bodily ramifications, sleep paralysis can leave a significant mark on persons who experience it. In this extensive analysis, we explore the varied effects of sleep paralysis, shedding light on its far-reaching implications.

Psychological Impact

a. <u>Worry and dread:</u> One of the most immediate and usual psychological ramifications of sleep paralysis is worry and panic. The experience of being unable to move or talk while being consciously aware can be unpleasant and even terrifying. Moreover, the vivid hallucinations that typically accompany sleep paralysis can heighten feelings of panic and helplessness.

b. <u>Sleep Disturbances:</u> Frequent episodes of sleep paralysis can impair sleep patterns and contribute to sleep disturbances. Individuals may develop anxiety around going to sleep, dreading the occurrence of future episodes, which can contribute to insomnia and daytime fatigue.

c. <u>Emotional discomfort:</u> Sleep paralysis can create emotional discomfort, resulting in emotions of anger, confusion, and even humiliation or embarrassment due to the hallucinations observed during spells.

Impact on Daytime Functioning

a. <u>Daytime Sleepiness:</u> The disturbed sleep patterns associated with sleep paralysis might contribute to excessive daytime sleepiness. Individuals may struggle to stay awake and attentive during the day, harming their productivity and overall quality of life.

b. <u>Impaired Cognitive performance:</u> Sleep deprivation induced by recurrent sleep paralysis episodes can impair cognitive performance, resulting in difficulty in focus, memory, and decision-making.

Relationship with Mental Health Conditions

a. <u>Association with Mental Health Issues:</u> While sleep paralysis is a sleep condition, it is also related with some mental health issues. Individuals with anxiety disorders, depression, and post-traumatic stress disorder (PTSD) may be more prone to sleep paralysis.

b. <u>Impact on Mental Health:</u> Sleep paralysis can further exacerbate existing mental health difficulties, especially anxiety disorders. The distressing nature of the experiences can lead to heightened anxiety, causing a cycle of terror and sleep issues.

Cultural and Social Implications

a. <u>Stigma and Misunderstanding:</u> Cultural beliefs and superstitions surrounding sleep paralysis can lead to stigmatisation and misunderstanding of the disease. This may result in folks feeling lonely or reluctant to speak about their experiences freely.

b. <u>Coping Mechanisms:</u> Cultural characteristics can also impact how individuals cope with sleep paralysis. In some cultures, unique rituals or practices are adopted to avoid or control sleep paralysis episodes.

Impact on Lucid Dreaming

a. <u>Lucid Dreaming Potential:</u> Some folks with experience in lucid dreaming may use sleep paralysis as a route to lucid dreaming. They may recognize the state of sleep paralysis as a dream and consciously regulate their thoughts and emotions to change the experience into a lucid dream.

b. <u>Lucid Nightmare Potential:</u> On the other side, for people untrained with lucid dreaming techniques, sleep paralysis can lead to powerful and unsettling lucid nightmares, making the experience much tougher to traverse.

Sleep Paralysis and Co-occurring Conditions

As discussed earlier, sleep paralysis can co-occur with other sleep disorders, such as narcolepsy and REM sleep behaviour disorder, or mental health difficulties including anxiety and depression. The implications of sleep paralysis may be modified or increased by the presence of numerous co-occurring disorders.

Sleep Paralysis and Quality of Life

The cumulative impacts of sleep paralysis on an individual's psychological well-being, sleep quality, and everyday performance can drastically degrade their overall quality of life.

The distress and terror associated with sleep paralysis can lead to unpleasant sensations and a sense of powerlessness, reducing the individual's pleasure in life and ultimately to social disengagement.

Sleep paralysis can also impair normal activities and affect performance at work or school. The combination of daytime sleepiness, impaired cognitive performance, and emotional distress can impede productivity and interpersonal interactions, adding to the load on the affected individual.

Sleep Paralysis and Sleep Disorders

Sleep paralysis usually coexists with other sleep disorders, such as narcolepsy and REM sleep behaviour disorder. The emergence of sleep paralysis can sometimes be an early indicator of an underlying sleep issue, recommending additional inquiry and diagnosis.

Additionally, the impact of sleep paralysis may be amplified when it occurs in conjunction with other sleep disorders.

For example, patients with narcolepsy feel severe daytime tiredness and may be more prone to sleep paralysis during abrupt sleep bouts. The combination of these sleep disturbances might result in more substantial interruptions to an individual's regular life.

Interference with Healthy Sleep Habits

Sleep paralysis episodes can interfere with the establishment of good sleep patterns. Fear of falling back asleep after a sleep paralysis episode may cause individuals to forgo sleep or change their sleep regimen to decrease the risk of subsequent occurrences. This can result in uneven sleep patterns, sleep deprivation, and greater sleep disturbances, repeating the cycle of sleep disruption and anxiety.

Impact on Mental Health Treatment

For people with co-occurring mental health concerns, sleep paralysis could impair the therapeutic process. The fear and panic associated with sleep paralysis may be misconstrued for symptoms of an anxiety disorder, leading to the misdiagnosis or insufficient treatment of the underlying illness.

Addressing sleep paralysis as a discrete sleep disorder and teaching mental health practitioners about its distinguishing aspects is crucial to assure full and effective treatment for persons with co-occurring diseases.

Chapter 8

TREATMENT OPTIONS FOR SLEEP PARALYSIS

Sleep paralysis is a confused sleep disorder characterised by brief muscle paralysis during the transition between consciousness and sleep or while waking up. While sleep paralysis episodes are typically harmless and self-limiting, they can be uncomfortable and emotionally distressing for people who encounter them.

Fortunately, numerous therapy alternatives are available to aid patients to manage and cope with sleep paralysis efficiently. In this extensive analysis, we look into the different treatment approaches for sleep paralysis, ranging from lifestyle alterations to therapeutic procedures.

EDUCATION AND REASSURANCE

One of the initial measures in managing sleep paralysis is providing individuals with precise information and comfort regarding the nature of the sickness.

Understanding that sleep paralysis is a frequent and natural condition could ease stress and anxiety related to bouts. Education about the neurophysiology of sleep paralysis can also help demystify the experience and minimise misconceptions.

IMPROVING SLEEP HYGIENE

Maintaining proper sleep hygiene is crucial for treating sleep paralysis and boosting overall sleep quality. Some key sleep hygiene habits include:

- Establishing a Consistent Sleep Schedule: Going to bed and waking up at the same time each day helps regulate the sleep-wake cycle and lowers the probability of sleep interruptions, including sleep paralysis.

- Creating a Comfortable Sleep Environment: A dark, peaceful, and comfortable sleep environment can assist better sleep and prevent disruptions during the night.

- Avoiding Stimulants Before Bed: Caffeine, nicotine, and other stimulants should be avoided in the hours preceding bedtime, as they can interfere with the ability to fall asleep.

- Limiting Screen Time: Exposure to screens (e.g., phones, computers, TVs) before bedtime might influence the synthesis of the sleep hormone melatonin. Reducing screen time before bedtime can aid in falling asleep more easily.

MANAGING STRESS AND ANXIETY

Stress and concern are known triggers for sleep paralysis episodes. Incorporating stress management strategies into regular activities can be useful in reducing the number and intensity of sleep paralysis episodes. Techniques such as mindfulness meditation, relaxation exercises, and deep breathing might assist manage stress and encourage relaxation before night.

TREATING UNDERLYING SLEEP DISORDERS

In certain instances, sleep paralysis may co-occur with other sleep disorders, such as narcolepsy or sleep apnea. Identifying and treating these underlying sleep disorders can assist improve overall sleep quality and lessen the frequency of sleep paralysis episodes.

MEDICATIONS

While there is no one medicine licensed especially for treating sleep paralysis, several medications recommended for underlying sleep disorders may indirectly help control sleep paralysis. For example:

- Selective Serotonin Reuptake Inhibitors (SSRIs): SSRIs are widely used to treat anxiety and depression, which can be associated with sleep paralysis. Managing these problems with SSRIs may lower the likelihood of sleep paralysis in some patients.

- Medications for Narcolepsy: For patients with sleep paralysis associated with narcolepsy, drugs such as modafinil or sodium oxybate, which are used to manage narcolepsy symptoms, may indirectly assist in reducing the frequency of sleep paralysis episodes.

COGNITIVE-BEHAVIORAL THERAPY (CBT)

Cognitive-Behavioral therapeutic (CBT) might be a good therapeutic choice for those experiencing considerable distress or worry due to sleep paralysis. CBT seeks to modify cognitive processes and behaviours that contribute to fear and dread, helping patients develop coping mechanisms to manage sleep paralysis episodes better.

<u>LUCID DREAMING TECHNIQUES</u>

As addressed in the relationship between sleep paralysis and lucid dreams, folks with experience in lucid dreaming techniques may use their lucid dreaming abilities to turn sleep paralysis episodes into more positive and empowering dream experiences.

<u>SLEEP SPECIALIST CONSULTATION</u>

For those having frequent or distressing sleep paralysis episodes that adversely impact their quality of life, consulting a sleep specialist or sleep medicine expert may be recommended.

A sleep specialist may offer a detailed evaluation, diagnose any underlying sleep disorders, and design a comprehensive treatment plan based on an individual's specific needs and circumstances.

HYPNOTHERAPY

Hypnotherapy is another potential treatment option for persons with sleep paralysis. Hypnotherapy comprises establishing a relaxed state of concentrated attention (hypnosis) to facilitate positive changes in ideas, behaviours, and emotions.

In the context of sleep paralysis, hypnotherapy may assist clients resolve any underlying anxiety or trauma linked with the episodes, lessening the emotional impact of sleep paralysis experiences.

During hypnotherapy sessions, a trained therapist may get the subject into a state of profound relaxation and use various ways to explore the emotions and thoughts related with sleep paralysis.

By creating a sense of control and confidence during the hypnotic state, individuals may get a better knowledge of their reactions to sleep paralysis and construct coping mechanisms to handle the episodes more efficiently.

SUPPORT GROUPS AND PEER SUPPORT

Connecting with those who have experienced sleep paralysis can be soothing and empowering. Support groups or online forums dedicated to sleep disorders, including sleep paralysis, provide individuals with a platform to share their experiences, seek assistance, and learn from others facing similar challenges. Peer support can help individuals feel less isolated and accept their feelings, making it easier to endure sleep paralysis.

AVOIDING TRIGGERS

Identifying and avoiding likely triggers for sleep paralysis episodes might also be beneficial. While triggers may vary from person to person, some common triggers include uneven sleep habits, sleep deprivation, and excessive stress. By recognizing and treating these triggers, individuals may minimise the probability of developing sleep paralysis.

RELAXATION TECHNIQUES BEFORE BEDTIME

Incorporating relaxation techniques into the bedtime ritual helps support a quiet and tranquil transition to sleep. Engaging in activities such as reading a book, having a warm bath, or practising light stretching exercises can help relax the mind and body, preparing persons for a more pleasant sleep.

SLEEP MONITORING AND KEEPING A SLEEP DIARY

Keeping a sleep journal can be a significant tool in identifying patterns and likely reasons for sleep paralysis episodes.

Recording factors like sleep duration, sleep quality, bedtime practices, and stress levels can provide substantial insights for individuals and their healthcare practitioners.

Sleep monitoring technology can also assist in tracking sleep patterns and identifying any underlying sleep disorders.

LIFESTYLE MODIFICATIONS

Making healthy lifestyle choices can have a good impact on sleep quality and general well-being. Regular physical exercise, a balanced diet, and limiting the consumption of alcohol and caffeine can contribute to better sleep health and potentially lessen the frequency of sleep paralysis episodes.

COMBINING MULTIPLE APPROACHES

It is crucial to note that no single therapy strategy works for everyone, and a combination of varied strategies may be most useful in managing sleep paralysis.

For instance, an individual might benefit from a combination of stress management measures, cognitive-behavioural therapy, and relaxing activities before night. Working with healthcare professionals, such as sleep specialists or therapists, can assist construct a detailed treatment plan based on an individual's specific needs and difficulties.
The management of sleep paralysis encompasses a comprehensive method that empowers individuals to cope with and minimise the impact of these occurrences.

From boosting sleep hygiene and stress management to studying therapeutic methods and support groups, therapy options for sleep paralysis are varied and adjustable to individual needs.

By understanding the available options and seeking appropriate therapy, individuals can develop a sense of control over their sleep paralysis experiences, leading to increased sleep quality and general well-being.

As research continues to shed light on the nuances of sleep disorders, including sleep paralysis, the science of sleep medicine is focused on providing effective and compassionate care for persons afflicted by this unique event.